RODGERS AND HAMMERSTEIN™

THE SOUND OF MUSIC

Music by
Richard Rodgers

Lyrics by
Oscar Hammerstein II

ISBN 978-1-4584-0514-2

WILLIAMSON MUSIC®

AN IMAGEM COMPANY™
www.williamsonmusic.com

EXCLUSIVELY DISTRIBUTED BY

HAL•LEONARD®
CORPORATION

7777 W. BLUEMOUND RD. P.O. BOX 13819 MILWAUKEE, WI 53213

Visit Hal Leonard Online at
www.halleonard.com

12

14

Edelweiss

Electronic Organs
Upper: Flute (or Tibia) 4'
      Sustain
Lower: Flute 8'
Pedal: 8'
Vib./Trem.: On, Fast

Drawbar Organs
Upper: 00 0600 000
Lower: (00) 7000 000
Pedal: 05
Vib./Trem.: On, Fast

Lyrics by OSCAR HAMMERSTEIN II
Music by RICHARD RODGERS

Slowly
R.H. 8va to end

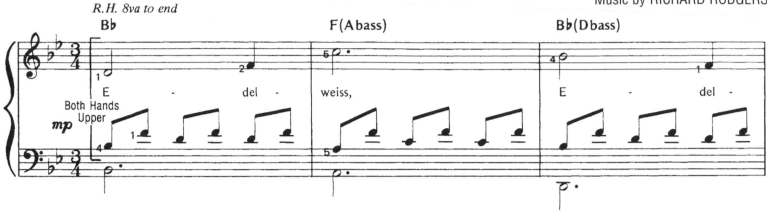

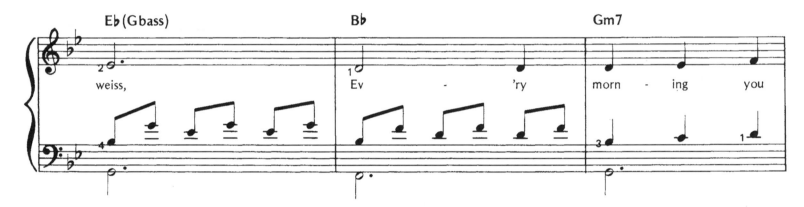

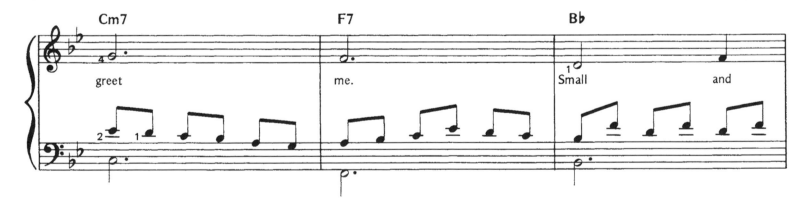

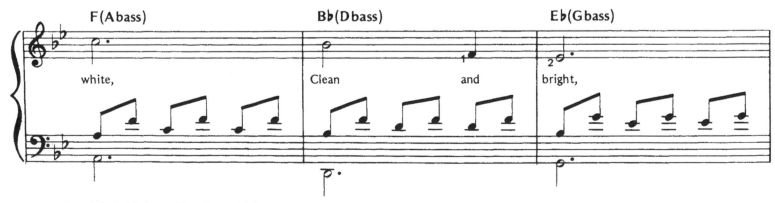

My Favorite Things

Electronic Organs
Upper: Flutes (or Tibias) 16', 8', 4',
          Trumpet
Lower: Flutes 8', 4', String 8'
Pedal: 16', 8'
Vib./Trem.: On, Fast

Drawbar Organs
Upper: 80 7766 008
Lower: (00) 8076 000
Pedal: 36
Vib./Trem.: On, Fast

Lyrics by OSCAR HAMMERSTEIN II
Music by RICHARD RODGERS

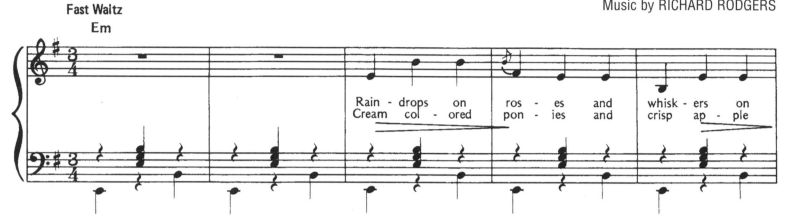

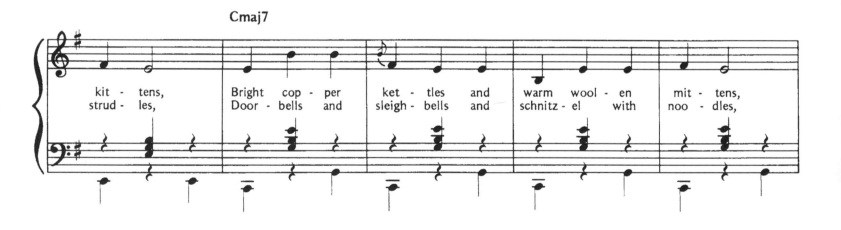

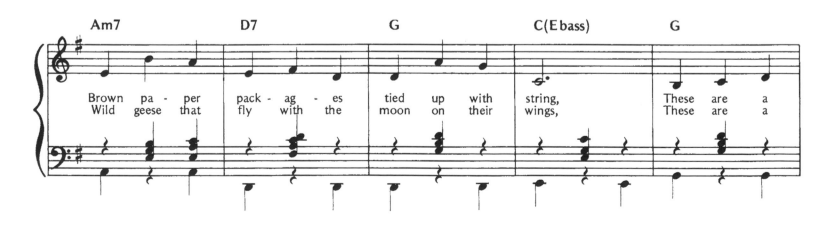

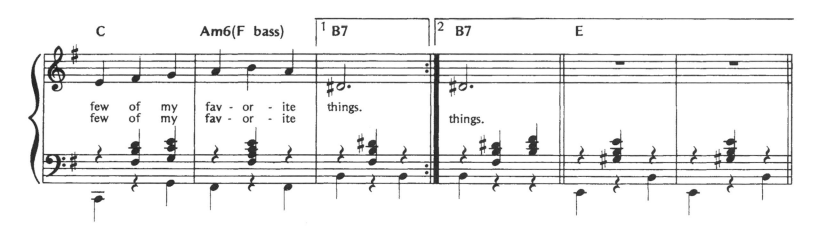

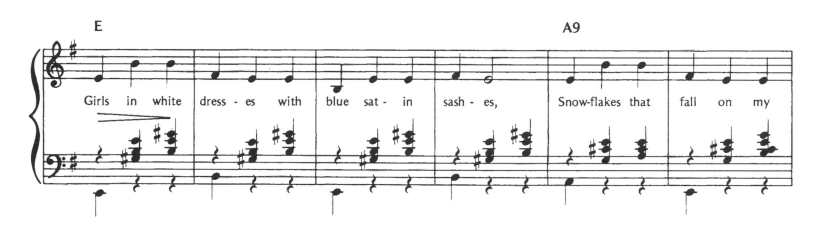

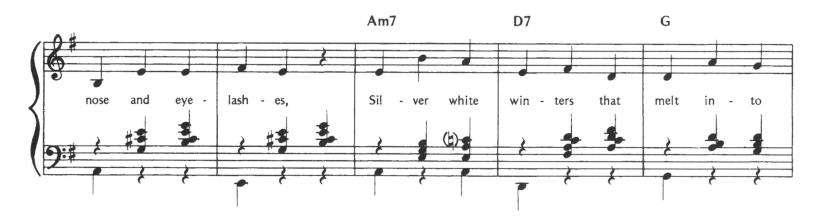

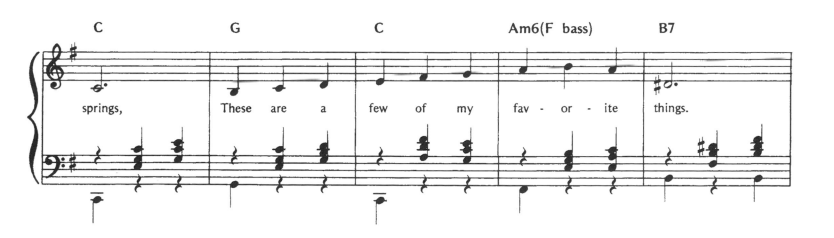

18

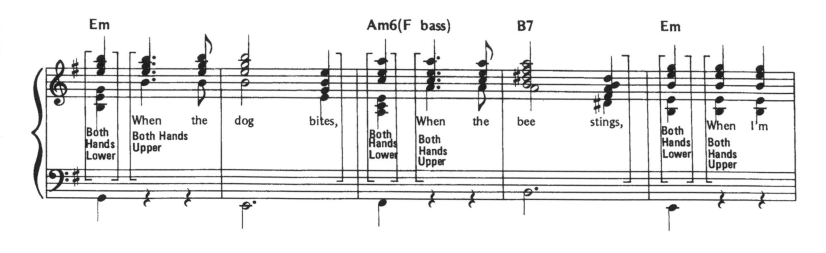

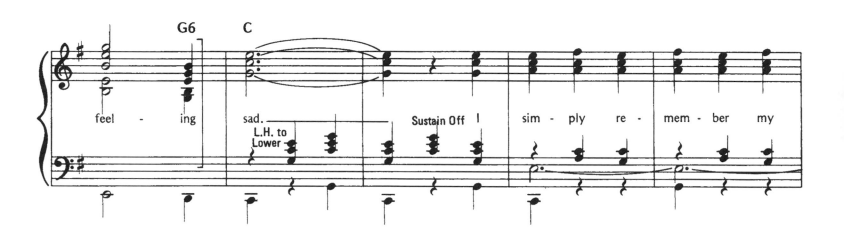

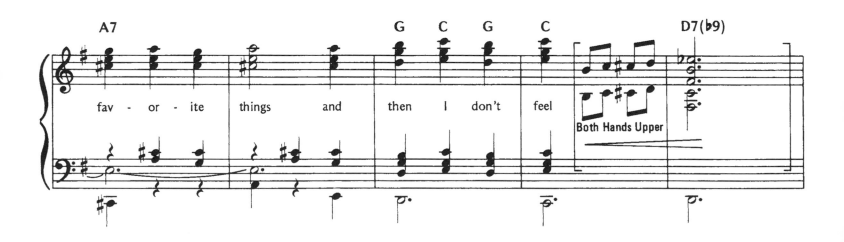

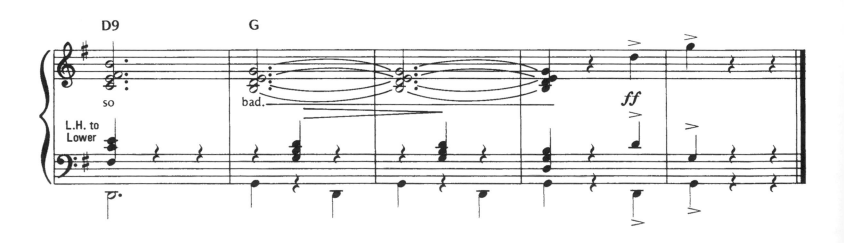

Sixteen Going On Seventeen

Electronic Organs
Upper: Flutes (or Tibias) 16', 4'
      String 8'
Lower: Flutes 8, 4', Diapason 8'
Pedal: String Bass
Vib./Trem.: On, Fast

Drawbar Organs
Upper: 40 8505 004
Lower: (00) 7634 212
Pedal: String Bass
Vib./Trem.: On, Fast

Lyrics by OSCAR HAMMERSTEIN II
Music by RICHARD RODGERS

You wait, lit-tle girl, on an emp-ty stage For fate to turn the light on. Your life, lit-tle girl, is an emp-ty page That men will want to write on, to write on.

You are six-teen, go-ing on sev-en-teen, Ba-by, it's time to think!

The Sound of Music

Electronic Organs
Upper: Flute (or Tibia) 8′, Diapason 8′,
  String 8′
Lower: Flutes 8′, 4′
Pedal: 8′
Vib./Trem.: On, Fast

Drawbar Organs
Upper: 30 8320 000
Lower: (00) 6501 000
Pedal: 24
Vib./Trem.: On, Fast

Lyrics by OSCAR HAMMERSTEIN II
Music by RICHARD RODGERS

Moderately, with expression